EMILY AS SOMETIMES
THE FOREST WANTS THE FIRE

Emily Poems, 2006–2018

Emily *as* Sometimes *the* Forest Wants *the* Fire

Emily Poems
2006 – 2018

DARREN C. DEMAREE

HB

in Chris
in 2020

First Edition, 2019
ISBN 978-0-578-51493-2

Edited by Gabrielle Lawrence
Cover and interior layout by Peter Barnfather

Cover art: *The Wind*, by Félix Vallotton
(courtesy National Gallery of Art, Washington)

Type set in Bergamo Pro, FontSite Inc.

Printed in the United States of America

Published by Harpoon Books
harpoonreviewbooks.com

For Emily

a woman too beautiful and interesting
to ever lose my attention

Contents

EMILY AS ...

Written by
William Elliot Whitmore 1

A Nasturtium Blossom
Fallen into the Ravine 2

A Mango Hitting the Ground 3

A Shadow Folded Four Times 4

An Answer More Convincing 5

The Firmament 7

The First Question
Is a Blood Question 8

I Hold Three of Her Shoes 9

A High Window 10

Honeysuckle 11

I Wanted to Know
the Purpose of the Rag 12

A Town, Earlier 13

A Strict Record of
Our Herb Garden 14

The Length of a Fox 16

Fall 17

A Pious Crowd & a Rabbit 18

A Leveling of Ground 19

Dart & Pivot 21

EMILY AS ...

We Never Learned
    Why the Scar Stopped 22
A Pin of Light 23
I Explained to Her Who the
    Photographer Kevin Carter Was . . 24
The Trajectory
    of the Armadillo 25
Underneath the Train 26
Elsewhere, Sunflowers 27
A Tire's Hot Squeal 28
A Love Poem Taken From
    a Chinese Take-Out Menu 29
The Air Trembles
    With Our Voices 30
Snow on Dark Water 32
Not Drunk, but by Love 34
A Choke of Silk 35
A Smile While Thinking 36
Thousands of
    Colliding Butterflies 37
Gloom We Shed 39
The Length of My Gaze 40
Imperfect Light 41

Circling Like the
    Sparrows in Early Evening 42
Erotica at the Table 44
I Ran a Very Long Way 45
Madden Me Fair 46
A History of Living Bone 47
A One-Act Play
    Written by Ted Brengle 48
The Rim of Night 49
A Brought Apple 50
Sometimes
    the Forest Wants the Fire 51
No Words 52
A Puma Crosses 54
We Bought
    a Parachute at a Garage Sale 56
The Plum Tree
    Takes My Pulse 58
A Ghost Deer 59
Almost Illuminated 61
Measureless 62
A Girl in a Chemise 63
An Armful of Flowers 65

EMILY AS ...

A Vacancy 66

We Discuss the Bullet
 We Found in the Backyard 67

By Choice This Time 69

Trees Remain Trees 71

I Slowed the Car Down 72

Debris & Sparkle 73

The Campfire
 Gathers the Branch. 74

Sometimes This Comes
 Close to an Attempt at Alchemy . . 75

Later, Jolted From a Dream 76

The Floor Wells. 78

I Hope for Another Garden 79

The Night
 Was Burnt Orange 80

Rockweed 82

We Keep the Doves 83

It Matters If This
 Is a Forest or a Ship 84

Written by Aase Berg 85

We Were Given
 a Room With a Balcony. 86

The Black Hood

    We Draped Over Our Faces...... 87

The Audacity of the Red Egg 88

She Discusses Her

    Own Body in Great Detail....... 89

A Bosc Pear 91

Our Lust Is a Common Lust 93

The Bird

    Swallows the Idea of Pain 94

The Ceremony

    Means so Little................. 95

It's Horrendous Really............. 97

The Proof Disappears 98

A Book of Endings 99

She Spent the Day

    Not Looking My Way 101

She Dropped

    the Lantern at My Feet.......... 102

A Smile Would Have

    Ruined the Picture 103

Where We Sigh 105

Acknowledgements 107

Emily as Written by
William Elliot Whitmore

The levy is an idea
& her shoulders,

that is a flood we
never could plan for,

but those sandbags
I kept around

the black locust tree,
they came in handy;

when Emily took me;
before she took

the rest of the town.

Emily as A Nasturtium Blossom
Fallen Into the Ravine

The wet narrowing
drove the darkness
into acceptance. It

was gravity, it was
a loosening of arms
from above the creek

& though we used
the rock-sides to cut off
the touch of the wind

& the touch of intimacy
there was no anguish,
no redemptive carry

of such beauty. A mile
down, at the bottleneck,
a shape of Emily emerged.

Emily *as* A Mango Hitting the Ground

If this were an orchard
how lovely it would be

if Emily fell from a tree
as the mangos fall, rolling

to the will of the root's
gradient. In Ohio, though

we don't grow any mango
& such a fall bruises deeply

what we had first hoped
would be light pat

from the dirt. Origin
of my fruit, I am sorry,

I did my best to imagine
a way for you to be unscathed

or cradled in good context.
I failed to simply catch you.

Emily as A Shadow
Folded Four Times

If one corner is paint
& one corner is blood,
the other two must be

precise in their passion
if there is going to be
a spark in the cement

of a disappearance.
Displayed, the beauty
is evident. As a trick

we must pay attention
to the process
if we are to see Emily.

Emily as An Answer
More Convincing

Emily says we are bundled in twilight,
fire-tested, survivalists with a wish
for death without elegy, a passing

of spirit that mourns only the physical
space a loved one leaves. Emily says
she will miss my body when I am gone,

she will miss hugging me, sleeping next
to me, leaving the children asleep in their
own beds in the morning, so our laughter

can naturally turn sexual. Emily says
if she dies first she will miss her body most
of all & I should be careful with her

ashes, I should make them important,
I should miss her body most of all, too.
We are young still & these things

make sense to talk about without sadness.
Really; it's just an overwhelming order,
a need to be adult, well thought out,

planned to mourn. Emily says she will
disappear over a hill at some point &
never come back. It won't be that simple,

but I believe she is right, we are all wide people,
tearing whole tides through a rapid sea,
& our departure will be lost in the surf.

Emily as The Firmament

Fragrant dark, devoted
to mirror the waters,
I picture your every star
as a lantern attached
to a rowboat, a separate
adventure taking place
at night with two people
not caring about being
lost, not caring about
the dimness or distance
of their light from anyone,
the flare out of their love
never reverting to gravity
or stories of human bodies.

Emily *as* The First Question
Is a Blood Question

Gathered to the rivering, I asked Emily
to sit in the summer dark, alone with me,
the parts of me that were her enemy

& in a field that held no crop, no rising
roots, she sat silently, listening to the water
flow away from us, the gravity of the land

like the future escaping & like there is no cliff,
only the waving arms that have left.
I had three words, a question I thought

could save us from joining the escaping
light, joining the puff of dust that rises
with the hard landing, I should have asked

her to quit drinking with me, so I could stand
to kiss her without hating her a little bit
each time she came home buzzed. Already

aware that only the water can carry you to
the bottom of the framing I asked Emily,
whispered towards the land, are you scared?

Emily as I Hold Three of Her Shoes

I would
write poems

about swans,
if I gave

a shit about
swans.

The swans
you're

thinking of,
do they

have anything
to do

with Emily?

Emily as A High Window

How bird, to gloss
only for the sky, to stare
only at the blue, to find

more blue when the cloud
collides with the glass
& to never give in

to the altitude. Look up,
farther up, that non-shatter
is exactly where she is.

Emily as Honeysuckle

The vines left a mark inside my fist
& the small beauty that could never
grow through our own bones

was left to circle the terrible depth
our skins accumulated over time
& many seasons of wanting more

time with beauty so close to the thick
crooks our bodies developed
as invitation. The flowers were subtle

& seemed hidden underneath
the untended growth by the garage
& we never doubted their small light

& we never doubted the many shapes
of flower Emily could be if I looked away
& I never looked away long enough.

Emily as I Wanted to Know
the Purpose of the Rag

Thin level of my best efforts, Emily
has moved the cloth all day, over wood,
over linoleum, over the black paint

already chipping from the new stove
& I have seen the serious circles
she tests against the twists & timber

of our belongings. For an hour, unforgotten,
Emily takes the style of the cloth to me,
rubs my whole body with it, chips

at the density of my day, the smoke
& flourish of my actions. As I admire
most of what is Emily, I ask her once,

to explain the purpose of such a terrible
spilling of filth onto one rag, onto my body?
Emily, as she does, stays with her love

& returns to the minor turbulence of the buff
& compression of my narrow pursuit. She
is gentle with her regard for my dirty work.

Emily as A Town, Earlier

There was a great industry
of Emily. It sustained whole

generations of men. Now,

there is mostly silence. There

is still Emily, one Emily
& she is still around, bright

& dynamic, new in old fashions.
Fingers dipped into the ovens

that once lit up the sky

of the town, I grow desperate

to make sure she never leaves.

Emily as A Strict Record
of Our Herb Garden

I love the absurd
color charts,
the plan of Emily

to create life
beneath our kitchen
window, where

the children can
learn & play
in the dirt

& the rabbits
become friendly
neighbors.

I love the absurd
stance she takes
with a broom

when the children
are sleeping upstairs
& the bunny returns

at dusk. My girl
looks nuts
with that broom.

It's good the children
have named the animals,
that way, Emily

has some names
to interject between
some glorious profanity.

Emily as The Length of a Fox

I haven't the time
to find a bluff
to overlook an expanse
& understand
Emily.
I am in the densest part
of the woods with her
now, the deep
where you touch
everything at once
& believe in the small
bits of your flesh
that you can predict
the next tree that will move
& the next animal
that will eat the next animal
& that shared breath
of meat
is as indelicate
as closeness can be.

Emily *as* Fall

Deer tongue in the creek,
the whiskey bottle meets
the red, darting flesh

as a surprise? The bloodroot
has all fingers in the water,
waiting for the hoofs

to break the grass ungently.
We lap, we lap, we lap
& take what is coming to us.

Emily as A Pious Crowd *&* a Rabbit

Living presence, so full of leg meat
& belief in the corduroy jacket
of a more modern Jesus, we tried

to make blood sausage
from the collection of rabbits
we found, chased over the water,

simple in a boat, we never came
up with enough clean flesh
to ferry ourselves back to shore.

I forget if we ever tried the bread
& I forget if we ever tried the fish
& I know, even lost, we ate well.

Emily as A Leveling of Ground

Across the snow,
the sea change of Ohio,
the axe splits wood

as an empty threat
to the whole world,
but then again, hands

can motion the life
right out of this thing.
Personally involved

in the end of the world,
what the living do;
is command the rags

& muscles to be easy
with pleasure,
to take the blanket

& pull it over all heads,
to kick legs
like a ornery child,

a knowing child
with a flat surface
to give in to an eyelid.

I found Emily,
that means I am ready
for the rest of you

to close your eyes as well.

Emily as Dart *&* Pivot

Asleep, never resting,
the humming lamb
of the wonder, of labor

& of cupping, springs
even in conjecture,
at the owl of fresh

desire. It is night
& there are no shadows.
Emily is waiting for me.

Emily as We Never Learned Why the Scar Stopped

The story is almost always
about when the cut started
to make the pain directional,

& if either of us cared about
what divided flesh we would
give each other a damn break,

but since we want most to know
what stopped the knife's edge
from tearing across the vital

points, we continue to press
each other on the details
of who put the bottles

of whiskey underneath
the furnace unit. Was it her
as a threat? Or was it me

when I used to threaten
everybody? If they were mine
I maintain, they would empty.

Emily as A Pin of Light

Yet women
are the moon,
elbowed,

cast in dark
as the context
for our light?

No. It is dark
all of the time.

Emily has spiked

the world
for me.

The fruit
of such air

breeds stars.

Emily as I Explained to Her Who the Photographer Kevin Carter Was

Emily says there is no acoustic
life, that even the read through
of life's events comes with enough

reverb to shake a house down
upon any family. What if we distance
ourselves from the darkness?

I asked her. The darkness is
the story. The joy is a respite
from the story, Emily says. I think

that might be wrong, I told her.
Then, she yelled, why the fuck did you
tell me who Kevin Carter was?

Emily as The Trajectory
of the Armadillo

For Lisa Jarnot

If a woman can be flush
enough to exhibit language
that belongs in a display

for tourists then she has
a real, American talent.
Emily once called me

a pussyfist, which I thought
was quite a dirty term
until she explained that I

abhorred violence towards
women, but I thought some
men needed to get punched

in the face. That was clever
of her, I thought, but I was
more excited to hear her

spell it out for me. It's spelled
like it sounds, which is practical
enough for any billboard.

Emily as Underneath the Train

Think of what we will see, Emily said,
It could be the whole country, she said.
We could live in a hundred different towns

& be a hundred different people
& love each other a hundred different ways
& if we ever find a diner with the perfect

piece of Rhubarb pie, we will stay there
forever, we can have a hundred children there.
Can't we just be robbers? I asked quietly.

Emily as Elsewhere, Sunflowers

I've traveled
to leave Emily

presents
in places

she might be
one day.

If she's never
there,

then the yellow
I've left behind

will grow
as a gift

to the places
that missed her.

Emily as A Tire's Hot Squeal

I am the road for Emily
& have positioned

my body as such, to be torn
up on the occasion
she has the energy,

or the bravado to do so.
No finery, I am left lonely
as a road when she doesn't.

Emily as A Love Poem Taken
From a Chinese Take-Out Menu

Orange chicken
with two spicy pepper symbols,
I'll take two of you
in one order. If it drips,
it drips. Deliver it to me
without using your hands
on my Styrofoam. You can keep
the mustard. We have
no safe word for that stuff.

Emily as The Air Trembles
With Our Voices

Mostly I failed
to alter the light
& the dark

of our considerable
tenement sinning,
our small, wrong

steps we loved
to take. We have
both
been awful,

but we gave that
spirit to the sun
& let it burn

everything we didn't
want to keep
as a souvenir

apart from each other.
Those things we hide
throughout the house

like they are bottles
of whiskey. In fact,
some of them are.

Emily as Snow on Dark Water

Down
& away,
both
sides
of the lake
a threat,

Emily
tested
the ice
to fight
like
everyone

else.
She almost
died
that night,
but she
proved;

she is not
everyone
else.
That naked
girl lost
a toe,

but that body,
in context,
redefined
the rest
of what
the world is.

Emily as Not Drunk, but by Love

The story is always of flight
& drowning, but I walked
past the bank of chestnuts

piled up by the animals
obsessed with symmetry,
& I was not alone

& I was not warm either
& my hands were so full of dust
that the thought of recreation

took them over. If my chest
had been a kiln I would have
reconstructed whole parts

of Emily, would have fused her
back together in the shape
of a woman, clustered

to rock, to take seasons
of me, measured, sober
& the earth would be still.

Emily as A Choke of Silk

Delicate beam, thickened
in celebration of an induced
vision, we have seen the barn

on fire, but the barn has never
been on fire. We have seen
the rivers emptied, but the sky

has only grazed our veins,
kissing them with degrees
of warmth. We have, with

each other, been shoulder
blade to shoulder blade
with death, but not once

have we given a name
to that world, the one where
we don't exist together,

the one where the names we
speak give us no safety at all.

Emily as A Smile While Thinking

Relit cigarette, first in four years,
I am reminded by the revolver
of your sweet peach of a world

& however much you give me,
a shake of proper fruit, you are still
the thing I thought might kill me

& that respect is why you are only
ash to me now. Emily,
you are the opposite of all that.

Emily as Thousands of Colliding Butterflies

Not as a bee, so close
to the ground, so nested

in the one, colored hive,

my love is a lunatic

with wings, a dynamo
in reds, in oranges,

no yellow.
From a blue
sky filled
with nothing

my love has taken
to darkening the sun

with the purest collision

of thundering color

& on impact,
the falling
of some wing.

Follow the grasses,
you will step on the parts

of her she had no need of.

Emily *as* Gloom We Shed

The blood is a shadow whispering
through the chemicals & the lack
of chemicals, which are the mass

that takes the sun away in the first
place. On the floor, we are the shadow
without reliance on any astral body.

On the floor, we are never projected
onto anything other than each other.
The sadness, like heat, rises without us.

Emily as The Length of My Gaze

We all know the distance
between my eyes
& the physical

boundaries of Emily
is the deepest level
of oasis. The truth

of the human heart,
the scotch
taste of it, that sway

is the real Emily. I see her
all the time. I stare. I have
no idea what created her.

Emily as Imperfect Light

Hand over the flame,
she has a mole on her
right ass cheek that is

fucking righteous
in the eyes of everything,
but the rest of her occurs

too slowly, not enough
& with very little
uncommon discussion.

Emily as Circling Like the Sparrows in Early Evening

Let us compare the bitterness
of the hour,

that time just after the cars
have all lined up

like a bad science fiction movie,
when we breathe only

as slowly as the expedient chafe
of our thighs in work clothes

that never size up well
on the way home. Arrived

& in a terribleness of nothing
but the absence of terribleness,

I look up into the new colors
of the escaping day,

I watch the sparrows circling
our house near the ravine

& I believe that though
the possibility of greatness is gone,

this day may, if Emily allows it,
be broad enough

for my shoulders to feel
only the consequences of home.

Emily as Erotica at the Table

Drop that napkin, let's let the melting cheese
be a call to arms, the tomato bread bowls
brimming with promise of more bread under-

neath the soup & your arms, Emily, tender
with speed as you desperately try not to spill
your favorite meal on the baby's developing

bald spot. I will ignore the older child, the girl,
if you can reach across the table, if you can wipe
the red promises from my cheek, as astray

with my intentions, I have made a mess with
the tools you have given me to work with tonight.

Emily as I Ran a Very Long Way

I ran a very long way for a very long time
& as I slowed to arbitrarily finish, I was
handed a medal for the goal of which I knew

was sacrifice, but what was being called
achievement. I ran a very long way for a very
long time & I as I did it, overdressed for them,

the crowd of the republic, I was given a medal
for my style of running not for stopping to run.
I ran a very long way for a very long time

& when I lifted my arms, exposed my ribs I felt
two hands adjust my ribs, stuff a brown, flat
medal against my heart, it was Emily, it was

reward, for when I lifted my arms I kept my legs
churning, I kept running, never knowing
what the medals meant, but knowing she knew.

Emily as Madden Me Fair

Furious at me, pregnant
again, Emily has had me
moving furniture, lifting
not dragging, because
the carrying is important
if I'm to remember this
experience, if I'm to expect
her to do this ever again,
our backs must be the same,
like a gang with matching
scars, the initiation
of a second child has spirited
that living room into myth
& tale. Tell my story,
make it Greek, make her
a siren, beautiful, on
the couch, leading me
to ruin, to the changing
rugs, piling beneath her feet.

Emily as A History of Living Bone

It is the ritual of the moon, to find
the crack in the barn's red side,

to shovel through the shallow, thinning
slats, to find the early leaf of a flower

that nobody planted
& nobody knew was growing so close

to the animals. Kept alive
& swept away from any grief, the hay

& feces are all part of the frame
& the glorious flank of every animal

that finds shelter there will learn with every
sinking day, that the comfort of the moon,

each petal it finds, warms them too,
their living bones

& here, among all that,
their history will be full, will be protected.

Emily as A One-Act Play
Written by Ted Brengle

Each stone
is waiting
for a hand,

a flesh
wall of light,
more fat

than pepper,
more give
than spirit.

Emily as The Rim of Night

Sloshed, those extensions, the lost
glossings of our desires
reaching past Emily, they hold more

above the rim of the night than they
should. Gravity of our own bodies,
when we swirl, woozily, like a bear

that lost in his pursuit of fresh honey
to a swarm of small pokes, we extend
our arms to be steady amongst

the scene of our own abstractions.
The best and most crushing moment
of marriage is to ask simply, Do you

want to have sex tonight? The answer
to that question is almost always
mostly empty. Even a Yes has

very little momentum behind it.
It's the No that has a great tenderness
to it. That soft No is tremendous.

Emily as A Brought Apple

Harnessed,
tongue to her flanks

we have run through
the sugarcubes

& yet, fire
to fire, we pierce

the skin of the apple;
because it was there

& our mouths were
nowhere near done

& as process is flow,
our race is done

& the roses,
her wreath, is on me.

Emily *as* Sometimes
the Forest Wants the Fire

It's always in the morning,
when the real quiet
kisses the bark ungently

& without bend or give,
a sturdy loneliness finds pause,
like a dancer in the tree-line

at sunrise, it will take great action
to resume our steps. Could it
be we need to run

from something, if only
to build a good lather? We can
call it dew, without panic.

Emily *as* No Words

I proposed to Emily
that I paint her
instead this time,

that just maybe
the metaphors
could give way

to the actual curve
of her stomach.
I said I want to pull

each sparkly bit
& have them act
as stars. You can't

invent the paints
that would require,
she says. True,

but if I can keep you
naked long enough
I explained

anything could happen.
This was when she
realized I held no brush.

Emily *as* A Puma Crosses

A day without the tan
rags of Ohio,
I saw Emily walk naked

across our front lawn,
she was drunk, aware
that we can't have drunks

in our house anymore
& without a single tear
or regret for her state,

she stalked our home,
moving faster, smoother,
without a look to the neighbors

that were lining up to see
the last bit of her girlishness
be swallowed up by time

& her inebriation. It takes
an hour for each drink
to vanish from our system

& at dawn, Emily knocked
on the door, still naked,
still a mother of two,

yet somehow more dangerous
than she had been before.
She napped all day. I didn't want

to shake her, for what if
she was still dreaming as a girl,
as a puma, without fear.

Emily *as* We Bought
a Parachute at a Garage Sale

The air favors
the prepared
& yet when
the original
owner said
that it didn't work,
that the sheeting
was all torn up
inside, we bought
it anyway.
Emily said
that she could sew
it up, that I could
learn the mechanics
of the chute
& then we will have
stolen the safe
delivery from
any height of heaven.
I asked,
are we really going
to use this thing?
No. No. Never,

she said,
it just looks like fun.
That's what you
said when I asked
you to marry me.
That was when
she kissed me, etc.

Emily as The Plum Tree
Takes My Pulse

I wanted the garden
to rest against
the extensions

of my own blood
& when it did
& when it never

relented, I knew
I couldn't die
alone. You will know

the body is mine
by the outline
of her weight

against my fading
energy, my chest
emptying to cradle her.

Emily as A Ghost Deer

Threat of a threat,
we are so afraid
of the exact moment

of our ending
that we hold company
like we hold brilliance

taken from nature.
We name company,
put it against our chest.

When company leaves
& returns the approach
is subtle, pale,

a different shade of alive
& here again!
Good company leaves

many times
& returns more often
than they depart.

Blue, against a sky
with many motives,
I know Emily

will always return
in one form
or in another form.

Emily as Almost Illuminated

Fine powder mixed
with animal juices,
I am dead on, her
high spirit is a nudge
towards being witness
to an explained world
where we vow only
to be smart, to be strong
for each other, even if
it carries a great risk
towards our temporary
swing through deep
gardens, deep mud,
water that is always.

Emily as Measureless

I know how
many hand-
lengths she is.

I do not know
how to stop
measuring.

Emily as A Girl in a Chemise

Oh reach
& reach
further back

to where
those breasts
become mine

again. To where
the couch
can be our Venice

because Belle
is asleep
in her crib

upstairs. Bird,
my language,
my love

& lust, I
got those fifty
more years

you wanted
in the best art
I have ever seen.

That paint
is fresh. That paint
is drying

because

of
the secret animal
in our oxygen.

Emily as An Armful of Flowers

I would prefer less beauty
between myself

& the light noise
of a stem rubbing

on your blouse. Ground
against the delight

of your roses, my chest
would stain your chest

with my intention
to limit the air between us.

Emily as A Vacancy

When we dream of candles
they are always lit. When
I dream of Emily, she is gone

& I have to earn her return
with enough light that fire
has been reinvented as a bird

with exploding wings. She,
without fit, returns casually
as the wind to the wick

& I again must invent a human
carrier of the flame. I dream
of stubborn wax, always burning

& an overdressed Emily, so
burdened by her clothes
that leaving is a real nightmare.

Emily *as* We Discuss the Bullet
We Found in the Backyard

Gasped like lungs
trying to exist outside
of a body, Emily

& I took turns holding
the unfired bullet,
saying nothing at all,

we passed it back
& forth without pain
or show or question.

I went back to mowing
the lawn, thought through
a thousand scenarios

that had answers only
in the possibility
of the chamber.

We own no guns
& we felt no better
prepared for those

that do by having now
a projectile of such great
intent. Emily kept it,

keeps it still, next to her
jewelry box, those things
too valuable to ever wear.

Emily as By Choice This Time

Delivered near the sweetgum
that grew without being planted

behind our cinder-block garage,

Emily and I found our aging

cat digging towards the root system,
inspired to learn the color

of such a deepening plant.
Two

hands, with bones almost as light
as wings, I joined in.

Emily sat on the bench beside
the fire pit and lit the first cigarette

she had lit in years. I asked her

about her actions, and she
asked me about my own. The cat

wandered away without answers.

For a while we talked about nothing,
but where we could replant the tree,

where it could be seen and continue

to grow to be seen. She tossed the butt
onto the bricks and walked away.

We agreed later on, after a hot afternoon

in the dirt, that a third child could be
something we would both really want.

Emily as Trees Remain Trees

Limited ascension, Emily
is in bed because she is
Emily. I had thought she was

other things as well. That
was foolish. The voice
you love cannot become

another voice. The tree
you mow around will always
have roots that reach

for the same overwhelming
fullness. Emily is in bed
because she is Emily.

Would I really want her
to be some other place?
Could I even find her again?

Emily *as* I Slowed the Car Down

I wanted to reach the forest
before the morning
took the danger away
& the light found us
being dangerous with each other
on land that several people claimed to own
& nobody has wired up yet.
Emily wanted the road
to be a path we worked our way through.
I was beating the weather
& I was beating the sun
& she saw me tallying all of that
& with her mouth
she made the marble clear
& we never reached the forest,
until she wanted us to.
We made breakfast together,
in the slight rain that tagged along
with us. We hiked closer to the clouds.
We talked for a long time
about what we could see in this light.

Emily as Debris *&* Sparkle

That point
without liquor
& lingerie,
the front door
of comfortable
love, that
is damn scary.

Emily *as* The Campfire
Gathers the Branch

Swimming deeper into the night, the softness
left the scene when we were able to form a name
for the fire, when we were able dip the flowers

from the garden into the fire without cause or care,
we knew then that all we had done was create
hunger and give hunger a name we could say

with smoke in our eyes. Turning away, cowardly,
I dragged my hand across my face to wipe the chase
of the tendrils to my sweater. Emily added more

wood the to the flame, she changed the shape
of the mouth in the pit, flushed the sparks towards
the cuff of our pants. She loves doing that shit.

Emily as Sometimes This Comes Close to an Attempt at Alchemy

Like there might not be a room
beneath the roof that is Emily,
I have done things, they would be

horrible things if they were not
done in the name of Emily?
Yes. There is an incredible

science to relationships, sacrifice
& sacrifice. Is it still a room
if it is devoured by reactions?

Yes. The smoke can be the whole
thing. You can be blinded
& blinding in one supreme action.

Emily as Later, Jolted From a Dream

There are giant bones
in Emily's dreams
& they hold up the giant legs
of giant people
& when they walk, each step
takes away the sharp-edged light
of Ohio
& each direction they chose
becomes nostalgic
for the simple foliage
& that is what Emily does
in her dreams: she plants
cheap bushes where giants
have walked.
That's beautiful
I tell her all of the time
& she says that she really wishes
the giants, with their legs
that can ruin everything,
didn't, each of them, have my face.
No matter, I tell her,
I think it's really lovely,
how you frame our world

& have a passion
to tend to everything
that I have tried to destroy.

Emily *as* The Floor Wells

There are times when the soul
of our house appears to yield
to Emily's height, her lack of it,

& I will see her be giant in one
room only to return to her slight
wave in another. If this house

clings to her needs, then what
place do I have in it? I could
make sure the house is kept

in good order. I could hold it
together and keep it able to raise
Emily up, like a gift that reaches

past the ceiling, into the shallow
firmament of Ohio. Neither of us,
the house or myself, are crazy

about these doors. I have a key,
of course, but we both know
it would never allow us to leave.

Emily as I Hope for Another Garden

That was the difference
between where my words ended
& where Emily planted
the absence of other people
in our lives. I used to drink
& that means I have no other
friends than the wife
that didn't leave me.
She decorated
our land
as if we were popular
& I waited for my first visitor
to arrive since I had to have my blood
pressure checked hourly.
I spent most of my time rolling
these curious, oval lights she hung
in our backyard. I would hold each
one like they were a pear
& when I felt very brave I would flip
the switch to be well-lit
in my own yard, where
I could be found by almost anyone.

Emily as The Night
Was Burnt Orange

I destroyed
the rose bed
to lift
the rose bed
to throw
the rose bed

against the almost
evening
& since Emily
was naked
in the yard
again,

I had wanted
to have
the color
of her body
be without
context.

She stood
out in the black,
for a moment,
before the roots
landed at my feet
& the blossoms
curled around me,

she was whole
& in conflict
with the beauty
of the everyday.
I wrestled that
moment for her.

Emily *as* Rockweed

Where she has hidden
& where she has grown
strong enough to breathe

through the practice
of forgetting sculpts
& never reflects the reality

of our world together.

Emily changed the tide,
without the tide knowing

& I learned all about that
when I was yanked to crumble
in the reversal of a water

meant to push me past her.

Emily as We Keep the Doves

in a carpetbag
next to the bed
& when we made

love attached
the bag to the ceiling
fan. We used to

release the doves,
let their ferocity loose
into the Ohio sky,

but then we learned
that if we gave them
a little bit of motion

that was enough
to give them real hope
of actual flight.

Emily *as* It Matters If This
Is a Forest or a Ship

After we brush all the bones, pick rocks
that we can shape into vocal cords, sharp
rocks that we can clear thick teases with,

daggers used to build the murmuring
into a mountain that can shine brightly
without fire in the sky, it doesn't matter

if our flesh is a language, but it does
matter what we used our flesh to construct.
If we hollow the scene, we will need wind.

Emily as Written by Aase Berg

I believe in the relative
success of the synapse
& if Emily wants to be

part of that crackling,
she will pop to join
me past the dimensional

leanings of her present.
If Emily is entirely real
& here, we will see her.

Emily as We Were Given
a Room With a Balcony

Art is open-aired
& Emily is art.
I have seen her breasts

swing from the street
& known I wouldn't have
to paint anything

ever again. I wrote this
poem only after
I took the blurry picture

from beneath her. I never
am able to quite frame her
without shaking.

Emily as The Black Hood
We Draped Over Our Faces

It was a new game
we'd never played before.
It took me an hour

to figure out that this
wasn't a game. Emily
wanted us to hide

with the near-holy silence
of our togetherness,
weighted down slightly.

If I was meant to say
God's name I ruined it
by whispering Emily.

Emily *as* The Audacity of the Red Egg

for Sam Roxas-Chua

The sun is never white.
The chest collects
only breakable bones.
Each new day
carries with it a tribe
so native to this
moment the wars
do not have the time
to fill our throats
with a second cry.
I look to focus my eyes
on the landscape
& the fog that once
hugged Ohio charges
me. I relax my gaze
& I see Emily
as a red egg, paused
on the impossible tip
of love. I see her
in defiance of all want.
A table cannot starve.

Emily as She Discusses Her Own Body in Great Detail

If you've been stabbed
you don't so much care about the knife
that stabbed you,

but once you survive
the upside down garden being flipped
around more

than a few times
every blade
of grass becomes real gospel.

I have seen Emily's body slip between
my ribs. I have survived both
her wrist

& the story of her wrist.
I have bled the way she prefers
me to bleed. She always smiles

when her hand drags
against the slight aging
of her weaponry.

I'm excited all the time
to hear the adjectives she chooses
to describe her violent attention.

Emily as A Bosc Pear

There is a true shape
displaced
& claimed

by the delusion
& the delusion's comrade
& if all that soil

still tastes honeyed
amidst
that claim

that all love is fruit,
then whatever
skin is leftover,

that is the skin
Emily is wearing.
She will

always be
a visiting blood
held together

by my poor
metaphors. She drips
& I call it juice.

She sings
& I call it a garden.
I open my eyes

& I know all
that's been ruined
is my understanding.

Emily as Our Lust Is a Common Lust

Seriously,
it's almost all
buttons.

Emily *as* The Bird
Swallows the Idea of Pain

Every cherry
has enough good flesh
to stomach a seed.

Emily as The Ceremony
Means so Little

The pleasure
just shuffles weight.

Emily stays
with me because

I am sober
& can cook dinner

for a family
of five.

I am never
late. All of my failures

are gentle.
The pleasure makes us

feel glorious
& whole in a room

full of light
sort of way,

but that pleasure
is just shuffling weight

around so we
can balance this

second act
with a joy we often

forget about.

Emily as It's Horrendous Really

Every refusal is generous.
Emily
says no

for me sometimes
& though I want
to say yes to everything

all the time,
her strength keeps me
bored, alive.

She wants me
much longer than
I've ever wanted myself.

Emily as The Proof Disappears

To taste
the displaced beauty of Ohio
is to dissolve

the whole of the valley.
We've been leaking
into Kentucky for years.

I love it
when Emily vanishes for me
to find her east of Lexington.

Emily as A Book of Endings

For Leslie Harrison

I chose Emily, because I knew
that if she chose me
I could prepare for death

in a way made my desperation
to keep living something tangible.
Now, with each child we have

I am cemented in the panic
of the living. Now, since she
keeps choosing me

every morning, I am able
to taunt mortality in a way
that will leave claw marks

in the fields of Ohio.
How glorious it will be
to be dragged from the living

& to scream one name, to spit
one name at my weakening
grip, to expect the strength

to return to me just like
the thousands of other times
I've used her name to live longer.

Emily as She Spent the Day Not Looking My Way

I am thawed. Deep
in winter, I am warm
for Emily

& she knows that.
The sky stays stark
& she knows that

as well. I am thawed
& I still invite her
to walk across me.

She prefers the shore
most days.
I can only be the lake

& most of my invitations
aren't landscape.
I am blue

stretched out
& I wait for her heel
to decide the season.

Emily as She Dropped
the Lantern at My Feet

I always wear cotton
just in case Emily needs me
to go up in flames.

I get to be the one that holds
her fire! How tender
of her to choose me

from the crashing to burn
just enough for her to lead
our children to safety.

How terrible it must be for a man
to have less of a purpose
than to be burned like me.

Emily as A Smile Would Have Ruined the Picture

There was one look, one picture
of Emily in a bathtub right before
we got married, she was travelling

with her family, she was in Madrid
or Paris or Istanbul, she had been gone
for a couple of weeks, so I had been

drunk for a couple of weeks
& she knew that I had been drunk
for a couple of weeks, so she sent me

a picture of her in the bathtub, one
breast covered, hair in a way I'd never
seen before, looking directly at the faucet

& so surely the tatters of my world
collected into a whole woman
so beautiful that when I got the picture

I accidentally deleted the picture.
I remember it clearly though, her face,
elegant, angry that she didn't have

her hands wrapped around the back
of my head to pull me off of the bottle.
She wanted to bury me in her beauty

& that almost worked too well.
I am sober. I don't have that picture.
I have Emily. She looks at me now.

Emily as Where We Sigh

I am not sad
nor am I languishing
here with Emily,

I just needed to let go
of that air that briefly
was supporting me

until she returned.
Chest without gradient,
I am free to join us

as the hawk joins
the simple sky
with great mission.

Acknowledgements

The Bad Version: Emily as We Discuss the Bullet We
   Found in the Backyard

Birds Piled Loosely: Emily as I Explained to Her Who the
   Photographer Kevin Carter Was, Emily as I Slowed
   the Car Down

Birmingham Arts Journal: Emily as Snow on Dark Water

Blueline – Emily as the Length of a Fox

Brevity Poetry Review – Emily as the Firmament

Brickplight – Emily as A Brought Apple

Cactus Heart – Emily as Sometimes the Forest Wants the Fire

Certain Circuits, Emily as A One-Act Play Written by
   Ted Brengle

The California Quarterly – Emily as A Vacancy

Cleaver – Emily as Dart & Pivot

Convergence – Emily as the Campfire Gathers the Branch

Cultural Weekly, Emily as Gloom We Shed

Dalhousie Review, Emily as I Hold Three of Her Shoes

Delmarva Review, Emily as It Matters if This is a Forest or
   a Ship, Emily as The First Question is a Blood Question

DIAGRAM, Emily as Where We Sigh

The Dirty Napkin, Emily as A History of Living Bone

Ditch, Emily as Circling Like the Sparrows in Early Evening

Ducts, Emily as Written by William Elliot Whitmore,
   Emily as A Choke of Silk

Diverse Voice Quarterly, Emily as No Words

Emrys Journal, Emily as She Discusses Her Own Body in
Great Detail

Festival of Language, Emily as A Ghost Deer, Emily as By
Choice This Time

Freshwater, Emily as A High Window

Frostwriting, Emily as The Rim of Night

Gambling the Aisle, Emily as the Air Trembles with Our Voices

Garbanzo, Emily as Madden Me Fair

Gravel, Emily as We Bought a Parachute at a Garage Sale

Grist, Emily as a Leveling of Ground

Hotel Amerika, Emily as She Dropped the Lantern at My Feet

Imitation Fruit, Emily as Underneath the Train

Indianapolis Review, Emily as the Proof Disappears

IthacaLit, Emily as A Pin of Light

Jet Fuel Review, Emily as the Audacity of the Red Egg

Limestone, Emily as We Keep the Doves

Literary Juice, Emily as I Wanted to Know the Purpose of
the Rag

Lodestone, Emily as I Hope for Another Garden

Main Street Rag, Emily as A Strict Record of Our Herb Garden

Midway Journal, Emily as Sometimes This Comes Close
to Alchemy

Olentangy Review, Emily as the Plum Tree Takes My Pulse

Origins Journal, Emily as a Posc Bear

Ozone Park, Emily as A Smile While Thinking

Parentheses Journal, Emily as It's Horrendous Really
Permafrost, Emily as Not Drunk, But By Love
Petrichor, Emily as Honeysuckle
Pidegeonholes, Emily as We Were Given a Room With
  a Balcony
Pif, Emily as Written by Aase Berg
Pouch, Emily as the Night Was Burnt Orange
Qua, Emily as A Puma Crosses
Rain, Party & Disaster, Emily as the Trajectory of the Armadillo
Really System, Emily as a Smile Would Have Ruined
  the Picture
Red Booth Review, Emily as the Floor Wells
Right Hand Pointing, Emily as Nasturtium Blossom Fallen
  Into the Ravine
Riprap Journal, Emily as Imperfect Light
Roanoke Review, Emily as Debris & Sparkle, Emily as the
  Black Hood We Draped Over Our Faces
The Round, Emily as the Length of My Gaze, Emily as
  Almost Illuminated
Sentinel Quarterly, Emily as Trees Remain Trees
Slipstream, Emily as A Town, Earlier
Spinning Jenny, Emily as Fall
Stoneboat, Emily as An Answer More Convincing
Studio One, Emily as We Never Learned Why the Scar Stopped
Sundog Lit, Emily as Measureless, Emily as An Armful

of Flowers

Talking River, Emily as Elsewhere, Sunflowers

Thrush, Emily as Our Lust is a Common Lust, Emily as
    The Bird Swallows the Idea of Pain

Timberline Journal, Emily as the Ceremony Means So
    Little

Toasted Cheese, Emily as A Tire's Hot Squeal

Tribeca Poetry Review, Emily as A Girl in a Chemise

Two Hawks Quarterly, Emily as Erotica at the Table, Emily
    as I Ran A Very Long Way

Twyckenham Notes, Emily as a Book of Endings

Up the Staircase, Emily as Later, Jolted from a Dream

U.S. 1 Worksheets, Emily as A Love Poem Taken from a
    Chinese Take-Out Menu

Vagabond City, Emily as She Spent the Day Not Looking at Me

The Vehicle, Emily as A Shadow Folded Four Times

Visions, Emily as Thousands of Colliding Butterflies

Yellow Chair, Emily as Rockweed

Your Impossible Voice, Emily as A Mango Hitting the Ground

Zaum, Emily as A Pious Crowd & A Rabbit

DARREN C. DEMAREE is a graduate of the College of Wooster, Miami University (MA), and Kent State University (MLIS). He is the recipient of a 2018 Ohio Arts Council Individual Excellence Award, the Louise Bogan Award from Trio House Press, and the Nancy Dew Taylor Award from *Emrys Journal*. He is the Managing Editor of the *Best of the Net Anthology* and *Ovenbird Poetry*. He is currently living in Columbus, Ohio, with his wife and children.

CPSIA information can be obtained
at www.ICGtesting.com
Printed in the USA
FFHW021439100619
52888333-58473FF